Doing social psychology

Doing social psychology

Laboratory and field exercises

Instructor's manual

Edited by

GLYNIS M. BREAKWELL
University of Surrey

HUGH FOOT
University of Wales Institute of Science and Technology

ROBIN GILMOUR
University of Lancaster

The right of the
University of Cambridge
to print and sell
all manner of books
was granted by
Henry VIII in 1534.
The University has printed
and published continuously
since 1584.

CAMBRIDGE UNIVERSITY PRESS
Cambridge
New York   New Rochelle   Melbourne   Sydney

THE BRITISH PSYCHOLOGICAL SOCIETY
Leicester

Published by the Press Syndicate of the University of Cambridge
The Pitt Building, Trumpington Street, Cambridge CB2 1RP
32 East 57th Street, New York, NY 10022, USA
10 Stamford Road, Oakleigh, Melbourne 3166, Australia
and
The British Psychological Society
St. Andrews House
48 Princess Road East
Leicester LE1 7DR

First edition published by The Macmillan Press, Ltd., 1982, as *Social Psychology: A Practical Manual*

Printed in the United States of America

Library of Congress Cataloging-in-Publication Data
Doing social psychology.
Includes index.
1. Social psychology – Problems, exercises, etc.
I. Breakwell, Glynis M. (Glynis Marie)   II. Foot,
Hugh C.   III. Gilmour, Robin.
HM251.D626   1987   302   87-6348

British Library Cataloguing in Publication Data
Doing social psychology: laboratory and field
exercises. – [2nd ed.]
1. Social psychology
I. Breakwell, Glynis M.   II. Foot, Hugh
III. Gilmour, Robin   IV. British Psychological Society   V. Social psychology
302   HM251

ISBN 0 521 34015 2 hard covers
ISBN 0 521 33563 9 paperback
ISBN 0 521 33564 7 instructor's manual

Contents

v

Contributors

Peter Ball
Department of Psychology
University of Tasmania

Glynis M. Breakwell
Department of Psychology
University of Surrey

Ray Bull
Department of Psychology
Glasgow College of Technology

Antony J. Chapman
Department of Psychology
University of Leeds

Mark Cook
Department of Psychology
University College

Hugh Foot
Department of Applied Psychology
University of Wales Institute
  of Science & Technology

Howard Giles
Department of Psychology
University of Bristol

Robin Gilmour
Department of Psychology
University of Lancaster

Rom Harré
Linacre College
Oxford University

Mansur Lalljee
Department for External Studies
University of Oxford

Bram Oppenheim
Department of Social Psychology
London School of Economics

Paul Robinson
Department of Psychology
Hollymoor Hospital

Robert Slater
Department of Applied Psychology
University of Wales Institute
  of Science & Technology

Mike Smith
Department of Management
  Sciences
University of Manchester Institute
  of Science & Technology

Peter B. Smith
School of Social Sciences
University of Sussex

Geoffrey M. Stephenson
Social Psychology Research Unit
University of Kent

Peter Trower
The Central Hospital, Warwick

Maryon Tysoe

Frances M. Wade
Department of Applied Psychology
University of Wales Institute
  of Science & Technology

Preface

This text complements the student edition of *Doing Social Psychology*. It is addressed to teachers who plan to use the exercises outlined in that book in their courses.

This instructor's manual explains what level of student knowledge is required and what materials are necessary for each exercise. Using this information, it should be possible to schedule the exercises to fit into the development of student skills and course syllabuses.

The basic exercises are suitable for students in their first course in social psychology. However, the exercises are designed to be flexible; for example, extra variables can be woven into the design and more complex forms of analysis applied to the data in order to make them suitable for advanced students. Exercises also can be modified to suit the specific needs and experience of each student group. One could even play the vivisectionist and cannibalize exercises: Several of the exercises fit together neatly. For instance, that on selection interviewing (Chapter 2) goes with the one concerning the effects of language on interpersonal evaluation (Chapter 6) and with the one concerning social skills (Chapter 8). Similarly, Chapter 13, on intergroup prejudice, complements Chapter 15, on group norms. In other words, the exercises can be treated as building blocks and linked together in a number of different ways, allowing each instructor to follow his or her preferences. The exercises, as they stand, have proved their effectiveness as basic teaching tools in the past, and they are also amenable to adaptation and extension to meet the changing needs of social psychology teaching today.

Glynis M. Breakwell
Hugh Foot
Robin Gilmour

Part I

Technique demonstrations

1   Questionnaire design

Robert Slater

Specification notes

Aim. To assist students in understanding the procedures involved in designing questions and questionnaires; to produce a self-administered questionnaire; by collecting and analyzing data (i.e., by piloting the questionnaire), to be able to redraft unsatisfactory questions (and answer formats); to examine simple hypotheses about relationships among variables.

Prior knowledge assumed. Little prior knowledge of the survey topic (smoking) is needed, but a basic understanding of sampling statistics (confidence limits for population estimates) and of 2 × 2 chi-square analyses would be useful.

Duration. It is an integrated exercise extending over two sessions (total of 6 hours), held some 3 or 4 weeks apart, with intervening data collection if the second exercise is done. The first exercise can be carried out by itself (3 hours).

Location. Both sessions are held in a normal teaching classroom or laboratory; data collection takes place in the field.

Resources. Pencils, erasers, wide-ruled paper, scissors, staplers, staples, scotch tape, blackboards, handouts on various topics, copying facilities (for duplicating questionnaires, etc.), pocket calculators, chi-square tables.

Special requirements. The second exercise cannot be done without prior collection of data. In order for such data collection to be done between the sessions, various demands are made on the instructor.

Participants. The exercises are appropriate for high school seniors and college freshmen and sophomores.

Value of the exercise

This exercise is relatively realistic, insofar as any survey into the smoking behavior of adolescents would probably begin with qualitative group discussions and/or open-ended, in-depth interviews with adolescents. It should enable students to examine the pros and cons of various standard question and response formats (see also Sudman & Bradburn, 1982). The exercise should also allow the formulation of questions in order to gather a spectrum of information, ranging from relatively simple factual data on age and number of older brothers, for example, to more sociological data such as ascertaining social status, obtaining psychological data on self-image and ideal self-image, or collecting data on discrepancies between thoughts and actions. Finally, the exercise should make students realize that although putting together a self-administered questionnaire is relatively easy to do, constructing one that is a precise scientific data collection instrument takes a lot of time and effort, testing and retesting.

Resources

The first session requires a room large enough for students to move from individual work to group work without much disruption of the class (each student will need a table or desk to work at, preferably with a surface roughly $1\frac{1}{2}$ by 3 feet). If it is possible for each student to have one table for individual work and one for group work, so much the better; otherwise, it is preferable for tables to be maintained in a group-work position throughout the session.

Before the session the instructor should prepare handouts on example question formats (taken, perhaps, from the appendix). Each student will need one set of such handouts. Students will need pencils and erasers (using pens and crossing out errors is to be avoided) and separate sheets of wide-ruled paper. At least one stapler and pair of scissors per group will be needed, plus spare staples and a couple of rolls of scotch tape. A large blackboard or other writing surface for the instructor must be available.

The above resources are those required for the first of the two sessions to be held 3 or 4 weeks apart. (The first can, however, stand on its own.) For the second session the instructor must be able to reproduce questionnaires, administration instructions, editing and coding instructions, and handouts suggesting further analyses of the data. Again a large blackboard or other writing surface for the instructor is essential, and two or more such surfaces may be useful (for when the data are being collated). Several electronic calculators should be available, as well as sets of chi-square tables.

Organization of the exercise

At the beginning of the first session the class should be told that the aim of the exercise is to produce a pilot self-administered questionnaire concerning aspects of adolescents' smoking behavior; that the 3-hour session will be held strictly to schedule; and that much of the time students will be working in groups. (If the second exercise is going to be done, this should be mentioned to students at this point.) The number of groups will vary according to the size of the class, but preferably each group should comprise no more than five students (otherwise groups tend to fragment into subsections, with one section working hard while the other watches, or worse!). It is useful to prepare a list of the groups, with members selected at random. Random selection makes the group-work process more realistic, ensuring more varied input of ideas concerning areas of the survey and enhancing, to a certain extent, the "testing" of items on people who are at least not likely to be best friends. It may be useful to point out to students that the grouping *is* based on random numbers selection and that the allocation to groups in alphabetical-order surname clusters is *not* random. The class should also be told that, where necessary, to keep to the schedule, the instructor will have to take some decisions out of students' hands.

Schedule

A detailed timetable is given in the Student Manual. Although there must be some flexibility in timing the various activities, the tendency will be for sessions to run over: It is very important not to let this happen with early sessions. When sessions seem to be coming to an end before their allotted time is up, however, move directly into the next activity. Some explanatory comments on selected steps of the exercises follow.

Exercise 1. Composing the questionnaire

Step 2. It is likely that in this and the next step a group (or groups) will find it difficult to reach agreement on the topic for the survey. Obtaining such agreement should increase students' involvement in the exercise, but it may be necessary for the instructor to impose a decision.

Step 5. Since it is desirable for each group to concentrate on one area, some areas of low salience may have to be omitted in classes with relatively few students.

Step 7. Attention should be paid here to retaining those facets that can be covered by collecting data through a self-administered questionnaire and to rejecting those that are likely to cause problems. For example, little seems to have been written directly on smoking and overt sexual behavior, primarily because people may object (on moral grounds) to data on sexual habits being collected and because it is difficult to relate what people do to what they say they do (a major problem in all verbal surveys about behavior). In step 8, agreed groupings of facets should be worked on by student groups other than those who originated them, so that students have a better feeling for the survey as a whole.

Step 9. Since this process could take a long time, if several groups are involved, the instructor should be wary of letting more than two groups use the rest of the class as subjects.

Step 10. In this period, different tasks may need to be delegated to different groups.

Step 11. The instructor should try to obtain rational consensus agreement, having heard the group's views, on the sequencing of question areas within the questionnaire.

After the session is over, the instructor should collate the material in the overall sequence agreed upon and arrange for it to be typed up and reproduced, so that each class participant can have a copy of the end product of the exercise. In writing up this exercise, students should be encouraged to review critically and constructively the questionnaire and the process by which it was constructed. They should examine questions for clarity and response formats for mutual exclusiveness. They should be encouraged, by way of formulating a general conclusion, to anticipate how respondents will react to the questionnaire in general and to each question or series of questions in particular.

Data collection

It is desirable that students give the self-administered questionnaire to some 10 subjects in order to see if their expectations about it as a data collection-instrument are realized. The subjects should be students/friends who are not drawn from the classes to which the full-scale questionnaire will be administered later. The data thus collected can then be used for redrafting the questions in the second exercise. However, it is better not to schedule this second session until 3 or 4 weeks after the first, in order to carry out the necessary preparatory work and to give students time to collect the data.

Preparation

Inevitably, the teacher will need to spend some time organizing the material collated from the first exercise so that it follows an internally consistent format. (If some of the material collated is considered not to be satisfactory for data collection, the instructor may want to use material from the appendix in the Student Manual and from the sources suggested there.) Having arranged the questionnaire in a presentable from – that is, one that can be handed over to respondents for them to complete – the instructor should write simple instructions to students on how to proceed with data collection.

Since students will be administering questionnaires between the two sessions, it is important for the written instructions accompanying the questionnaires to be comprehensive. The instructions should direct students to inspect a copy of the questionnaire and to make a note of any queries they themselves have about it or anticipate that respondents might have. It should be emphasized that when students administer the questionnaire they should be very familiar with its contents and have prepared answers to the sort of questions they think the respondents might raise. They should be instructed to make a note of actual problems with the questionnaire that do arise when respondents are completing them. These instructions to the students, together with the questionnaires, should be reproduced and collated in sufficient numbers for each student to administer the questionnaire to some 10 subjects with the designated same characteristics. Since these may well be peers, it might, on the one hand, be simplest to allow students to find their own subjects. This, of course, would facilitate the faking of responses. On the other hand, it may well prove administratively very difficult (although more desirable) to arrange for students to collect the data by administering the questionnaire to other classes in the school or college. The instructor will have to decide which is the more appropriate method of collecting the data, given the particular circumstances and the interval between the two sessions.

Administration

Students should be instructed to check that each questionnaire is complete (no missing or blank pages) and that pages are in the right sequence. Each questionnaire should be given a unique identification number that can be linked to the student who administered it. Each student should have two or three extra questionnaires for emergency use.

Students will need to be informed of the arrangements for administering the questionnaires. If they are being given the responsibility of finding appropriate subjects, the defining characteristics of the sample population must be told which classes they are to be using, where they are located, and at what time they are to administer the questionnaires. Obviously the instructor will have to have made arrangements well in advance with other teachers for them to cooperate. These teachers should have been fore-warned of the arrival of the students at such and such a time, that admini-stering and collecting the questionnaires will take approximately 15 to 20 minutes, and that with large classes two or more students may arrive to carry out the questionnaire administration. With classroom administration, at least 2 students should be present for every 20 respondents, in order to help issue the questionnaires, answer queries about questions, and collect the questionnaires.

Exercise 2. Revising the questionnaire and analyzing the data

Step 2.   During the session it might be useful to try to get feedback about problem questions that were noted when the data were collected, so the students will be wary of them in any subsequent analysis.

Step 5.   If possible, the emphasis should be on analyses that will help in the revision and improvement of the questionnaire.

Step 6.   The instructor should attempt to obtain consensus agreement concerning which analyses to do first. It may be decided that more time should be spent examining the implications of the descriptive findings, to improve the questionnaire.

Step 7.   Any analysis of data in this raw form is always very tedious and will show students the need to transform the data so that items can be readily analyzed by computer.

Having agreed on the method of the first analysis (for practical purposes a simple 2 × 2 chi-square table might be most appropriate), the question-naires should be sorted into the appropriate (four) piles and counted, and the contingency table should be produced. For example, in a sample of 100 female respondents there may be 27 female smokers (GS) whose mothers smoke (MS); 23 female nonsmokers (GNS) whose mothers smoke; 10 female smokers whose mothers do not smoke (MNS); and 40 female non-smokers whose mothers do not smoke. This would produce the following contingency table:

	GS	GNS	Total
MS	27	23	50
MNS	10	40	50
Total	37	63	100

Step 8. The contingency table should be set up on the blackboard, to-gether with instructions on how to calculate chi-square.

Step 12. Another way to do the three different analyses in the last six steps is to collate material in steps 2 and 3 in a grouped form for both males and females, "older" and "younger" respondents, and so forth. This would result in more chi-square analyses being done in the last half of the session by individual students, who can then have the choice of variables to relate to the variable on which the grouping has been based. If the instructor uses this strategy, a lot of calculators will have to be made available. It will also, if desired, permit a closer examination of the implications of the descrip-tive results for redesigning the questionnaire.

Students should be given a handout by the instructor suggesting further analyses of the data (prepared before the exercise). The instructor should collect the edited questionnaires and point out to the class the need for access to a computer for fast and effective analyses of data of this type.

As will already have become clear, if only the first session is held there will be no data available for analysis, except for students' opinions con-cerning how the questionnaire may still need to be modified. If the second session is held, the data will take the form of coded numerical information for perhaps some 20 to 30 variables for some 150 to 350 respondents. During the second exercise, therefore, each student will have a set of the pooled data for the survey from which a descriptive account of the responses to the survey can be given. Besides the chi-square analyses, students will not be able to pursue, with their simple frequency-count data, any further analyses that relate one variable to another, although they might attempt to determine whether selected frequency distributions obtained differ significantly from the theoretical distributions.

If instructors have access to a data preparation service that will produce computer data files directly from well-edited and coded questionnaires, and if they are familiar with SPSS-X (or a similar package) and have access to it, setting up multivariate analyses and more simple ones like cross-tabulations will be relatively easy. The kinds of data likely to be collected are suitable for a variety of forms of statistical analysis and can be used to illustrate many statistical procedures.

Discussion

The construction of the questionnaire in the first session will have been done rather quickly, and even though the instructor may have utilized some of the material in the appendix or from the references to collect the data for the second session, probably certain questions will turn out to be unsatisfactory (vague, biased, ambiguous, etc.) and some answer alternatives will also be unsatisfactory (unclear, not mutually exclusive, etc.). Such limitations should be pointed out by the instructor (and ideally by the students themselves) as part of the pedagogic exercise; otherwise the exercises might, unfortunately, reinforce the common belief mentioned at the beginning, that anyone can string a few questions together into a questionnaire. Students should throughout be encouraged to be critical of the material they are producing and be helped to realize that in a full-blown survey, with a relatively large-scale pretest (some pertinent questionnaires have been *piloted* on as many as 1,180 teenagers), much time and effort is put in by a great many individuals proficient in the stages of conducting a survey and analyzing the results.

Reference

Sudman, S., & Bradburn, N.M. (1982). *Asking Questions: A Practical Guide to Question-naire Design*. San Francisco: Jossey-Bass.

2   Personnel interviewing: a mini–training program

Mike Smith

Specification notes

Aim. To improve students' skills in the professionally important task of job interviewing. Subsidiary aims are to provide insights into training techniques and person perception.

Prior knowledge assumed. No prior knowledge of interviewing is required. Prior knowledge of training techniques and theory of person perception is helpful but not essential.

Duration. Between $2\frac{1}{2}$ and 3 hours. Students need to complete an application form in advance. Time available can be divided into hourly segments. The program is divided into four exercises each of which has five elements: (1) an introduction by the teacher; (2) a handout covering the instructions given in the introduction; (3) a role-play that is recorded on videotape; (4) a replay with feedback and comments from the teacher; (5) completion of a checklist to summarize the major points. Time available can be divided into hourly segments.

Location. For a group of 18 students, a large, flat (i.e., not tiered) lecture room would be sufficient. If possible, small rooms for groups of three students to use in practicing the exercise would be useful but not essential.

Equipment. Closed-circuit television (CCTV) with playback is highly desirable but not essential. A more sophisticated system involving three cameras, a mixer, and a special effects generator can be very useful. Duplication of nine one-page handouts is desirable.

Special requirements: None.

11

Resources

For the fairly typical situation with a group of 18 students, the following materials are required and should be reserved 2 or 3 weeks in advance.

1. Large-screen television
2. Tape recorder, tape, and take-up reel or cassette
3. Microphones, camera (with zoom facility), tripod, and extension lead
4. One set of documentation for each student, as given in appendixes 1 through 9 of the Student Manual
5. Four or 5 file cards
6. Two stopwatches

Read through the theoretical section of the Student Manual and appropriate texts on management or person perception, if these topics are to be included in the discussion period (e.g., Landy, 1985, or Smith & Robertson, 1986). The instructor should also be familiar with the closed-circuit television equipment and may want to prepare overhead projections for use in the introductions.

The format and schedule for the program are as shown in Table A. Note that the times for the components are maximum times.

Table A. *Schedule for exercises*

Activities	Total time (minutes)
General introduction to personnel interviewing	2
Exercise 1. Openings and closings	22
Introduction (7)	
Role-play (5 for preparation and 4 for role-play)	
Replay and discussion (6)	
Exercise 2. Covering the major points	46
Introduction (5)	
Preparation (6)	
Role-play (15)	
Replay and discussion (20)	
Exercise 3. Making them talk	55
Introduction (5)	
Preparation (5)	
Role-play (20)	
Replay and discussion (25)	
Exercise 4. Making a decision	40
Introduction (5)	
Preparation (0)	
Interviews (25)	
Discussion (10)	

Exercise 4 is handled differently. It begins with the traditional introduction (5 minutes), but preparation time is not required, since preparation for previous exercises can be utilized. Volunteers are obtained, and without attracting attention the interviewee should be handed a card saying:

For the first half of the interview, answer with a single word whenever possible; in the second half, give long-winded answers. Mumble incoherently at least three times. Try to give answers that are consistent with the referees' comments, which will be read out. Do not reveal these instructions until you are told to do so.

Immediately before the mock interview starts, the instructor announces to the whole group that a reference has been received from the principal of the candidate's high school. It reads:

The candidate is shy and very modest. The candidate has an IQ of 130, but this was not reflected in his/her SAT scores, which were around 1,000. Just before taking the SAT exams the candidate had been in the hospital. Although unable to swim, the candidate had jumped into a lake to help someone in a rowboat who was in trouble. Unfortunately, the candidate was injured and nearly drowned. Later a local society awarded him/her a medal for bravery, and an article about the incident was in last Sunday's paper.

The role-play (25 minutes) proceeds in the same way as previous role-plays, except that at the end the interviewers are asked to decide whether to hire the interviewee. When they have given their answer, the interviewers should be asked to give their evidence and the reasoning behind their decision (2 minutes).

A replay of the videotape is not necessary for the final exercise; the discussion (10 minutes) should focus upon the validity of the evidence and inferences used in arriving at a decision. At this point, the discussion can be widened to discuss problems of job interviewing in industry (some students can be asked to relate their own experiences). A good way to end the session is to focus on the training aspects and ask how interviewer training in industry would differ from the training just given (e.g., participants would have less theoretical background but more practical experience; more practice would be given to produce overlearning; and efforts would be made to assist transfer from the training situation to the factory floor or boardroom table).

Variations in method

The program can be amended to suit a wide variety of situations. In situations where *fewer resources* are available, the exercises can be run without a closed-circuit television system: The students simply make notes as they observe the role-plays. In this situation the time requirement is reduced by about 45 minutes.

In situations where *more resources* are available, an improved closed-circuit television system can be used. An ideal system requires two static cameras, plus one camera with automatic pan and tilt. The output of the cameras is relayed to a mixer and an effects generator with split-screen facility. In this ideal setting (show in Figure A), one of the static cameras is focused on the interviewee, while another static camera is focused on the interviewers. The instructor and the remaining students who are not involved in the role-play observe from an adjacent area where the instructor records events, switches from camera to camera, and manipulates the remote control camera. Perhaps the observers could watch the role-play through a one-way mirror.

If enough room is available, the students can divide into groups of three and, while one group's interview is being recorded on video tape, the remaining groups can perform their own role-play and regroup to watch the video. Inevitably, the additional organization requires additional time.

Additional time could also be used to explore models of decision making. Work sheets could be prepared to ask for the traits that interviewers in the final exercise use to decide whether to hire the candidate. The work sheets could also ask for the importance of these traits. The information

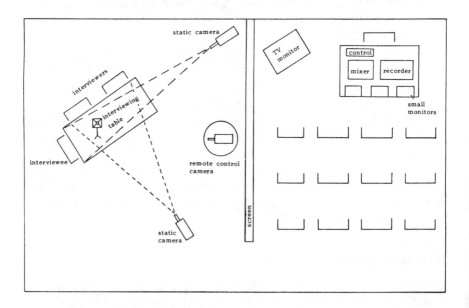

Figure A. Ideal arrangements for interviewing exercise.

could then be used to demonstrate the additive model, the averaging model, and the weighted averaging model of person evaluation (see Gergen & Gergen, 1981, p. 60).

References

Gergen, K.J., and Gergen, M.M. (1981), *Social Psychology*. New York: Harcourt Brace.
Landy, F. J. (1985). *Psychology of Work Behaviour*, 3rd ed. Homeward, Ill.: Dorsey Press.
Smith, M.J., and Robertson, I.T. (1986). *The Theory and Practise of Systematic Staff Selection*, London: Macmillan.

3   Attitude measurement

Bram Oppenheim

Specification notes

Aim. To introduce students to attitudes and their measurement by constructing a Thurstone Attitude Scale and to give them an understanding of the practical and theoretical issues involved.

Prior knowledge assumed. Little background theoretical knowledge is assumed, but a basic knowledge of statistics would be useful (e.g., measurement scales, item statistics, coefficients of reliability and validity).

Duration. Two laboratory sessions of around $2\frac{1}{2}$ hours each, plus a prior introductory lecture.

Location. The exercise can be conducted in a normal classroom or teaching laboratory.

Resources. Blackboard, paper, writing materials, rulers, a set of percentage tables or a pocket calculator, a set of ogive graphs, and envelopes are required. Some secretarial assistance would be extremely useful in preparing materials.

Running the exercise

The exercise is a fairly extensive one and requires a fair amount of instructor involvement in preparation and supervision, spread over three sessions. To summarize, the exercise involves three phases: (1) an initial session in which the instructor introduces the subject and the problems in it, setting a topic, and arranging for attitude items to be generated; (2) a first laboratory session, where items are judged and item statistics analyzed; and (3) a second laboratory session where a Thurstone scale is constructed. Extensive guidance in procedure is given in the Student Manual, but students are likely to need help with the material, as well as more extensive discussion of a number of the points raised.

Preparation

The instructor should read through the exercise in the Student Manual and prepare an introductory lecture, explaining the issues and elaborating as much as you think is necessary for the class to grasp the subject and to be able to carry out the exercise effectively. It would also be useful at this point to make up some suitable scale topics for agreement by the class and possibly also to arrange for copies of existing attitude scales to be available (e.g., see Shaw & Wright, 1967). Assistance from secretaries or possibly from volunteers among the students is going to be extremely useful, and this should be set up in advance.

Before the first laboratory session, items generated by students need editing, typing, and duplicating. A set of ogive graphs (see Student Manual, appendix 1) is needed, with as many graphs as there are items in the item pool, plus some spares.

Finally, a working schedule should be drawn up at the beginning. After the introductory session, the students will need a few days to absorb the material, do some interviews, and write the attitude statements. After these have been handed in, there must be adequate time for the item pool to be examined by the instructor to identify the items to be typed and duplicated and for copies of the item pool to be cut up into item slips for each student. After the first laboratory session, the second session can follow almost immediately or whenever convenient for the class.

Procedure

Introductory lecture

Instructor introduces the exercise, discusses issues involved in attitude measurement (see the introduction in the Student Manual). A suitable topic for the attitude scale is agreed upon with the class, and students are given information about writing attitude statements (students should be urged to do some interviewing before writing statements). A firm date by which all statements must be handed in should be announced, and then students should be sent out to generate attitude statements.

After collecting attitude statements from students at the agreed time, the instructor should edit and assemble the item pool to eliminate duplications and near duplications, colloquialisms and poor grammar, and illegible items, but the instructor should *not* leave out items that are ambiguous, double-barreled, lengthy, too cognitive, or that show some of the many other characteristics of "bad" attitude items. Students will learn more if such items are included in the item pool and then show up poorly in the scaling procedure. The item pool should then be assembled in random order and the items numbered on the left-hand margin. The item pool should then be typed, and duplicated twice. One set should be assembled as a test booklet or questionnaire; the other set should be cut up into item slips (one set of slips of the complete item pool for each student, in separate envelopes).

First laboratory session

The teacher should briefly go over the steps in the Thurstone procedure (where necessary, taking examples from some other attitude topic). After that, the envelopes with the item slips should be handed out. Put a horizontal line on the blackboard representing the attitude continuum, with 11 intervals clearly marked, from 1 at the left to 11 at the right, with the central point indicating a neutral category. The class should now agree about labeling the *favorable* and *unfavorable* ends of the continuum. Remind the students that these labels must be held to consistently.

Next, students should be intructed to ignore their own attitudes and to act solely as item judges. Each item must, as far as possible, be placed in one of the 11 categories according to its content, by asking where someone who agreed with the item would stand, in terms of *favorable* or *unfavorable* on the attitude continuum. When the task has been completed, students should enter on each slip, in the right-hand margin, the category number in which it has been placed, from 1 to 11. After that each student should reassemble the item pool slips in their numerical order, from 1 to 60 or 70, or however many items are in the pool, and return them to their envelope. (Alternatively or in addition, you might like to hand out written instructions, such as those on p. 128 of Oppenheim, 1966).

This judgment process can be quite time-consuming and often produces wide individual differences in working speed. The instructor might encourage early finishers to help slower students with the numbering and item sorting but *not* with the actual judgment process. Move around the class, making sure that students have enough working space, helping with queries, and checking to see that they are not reversing the direction of the continuum: that is, writing 8 or 9 when they should write 4 or 3, and so on.

While students are still entering their judgments, the instructor should put on the blackboard (1) a percentage table for the number of judges in the class, rounded off to whole percentages, and (2) an empty table showing the item numbers down the side (running from 1 to 60, 70, or whatever) and two headings across the top: "Median" and "Semi-interquartile Range" (SIQ). You may also want to draw a sample of the ogive graph (see Student Manual, appendix 1) on the board, with a worked cumulative frequency example (see Student Manual, Table 3.1). At this point the instructor should also divide the number of items by the number of students, in order to decide how many items to give each student for the item analysis.

Once all students have made their judgments, entered them on the item slips, and reassembled the slips in numerical order, allocate items to each student. Explain how to generate the two item statistics – that is, median and SIQ for each item – showing them how these values can easily be worked out with the aid of a percentage table and an ogive graph, and following the procedure outlined in the Student Manual. Working out an example on the board would help at this point. Students are then asked to calculate and graph the item statistics for each of the items allocated to them and then enter them in the relevant positions in the table on the blackboard. In the meantime you can help students who have difficulties, deal with missing values, and so on.

The instructor should now hand out the item pool booklets and ask students to copy the whole table of item statistics from the blackboard. You should keep a copy of the table of item statistics. Students should be instructed to bring their item booklets and the graph of item statistics along to the next session.

Second laboratory session

This session can proceed as described in the Student Manual, with guidance from the instructor, and should result in the construction of a Thurstone scale, even if not a complete one. Unless the exercise is extended, the class will probably not be able to compute a reliability coefficient, but you can present different methods of calculating reliability, as well as the possibility of developing two parallel scales from the same item pool. Likewise, the class will not be in a position to calculate a validity coefficient, but problems of validation should be introduced and discussed in relation to different types of validity. The scoring procedure should also be discussed: for example, the loss of information by not scoring the "disagree" responses.

Finally, a broader discussion can be started – on the Thurstone procedure, on attitude scaling in general, and on what such methods of measurement can tell us about the attitude domain under consideration. The "Results and Discussion" section of the Student Manual will provide a basis for much of this discussion, and the instructor can explain and elaborate on the various points where necessary. You may want to have available, as illustrations, some published examples of the use of attitude scales in both practical and theoretical research.

References

Oppenheim, A. N. (1966). *Questionnaire Design and Attitude Measurement*. New York: Basic Books.
Shaw, M. E., & Wright, J. M. (1967). *Scales for the Measurement of Attitudes*. New York: McGraw-Hill.

4   Social interaction: an observational analysis

Hugh Foot

Specification notes

Aim. The exercise is designed to teach students some of the problems associated with observing and recording social interaction. Students are trained in the use of a modified version of Bales' Interaction Process Analysis, and they use the system to analyze interactions in conflict and nonconflict problem-solving discussion groups.

Duration. Two 3-hour sessions are recommended: the first for training and data collection, the second for data analysis. If training is omitted, the exercise can be compressed into one session of 3 hours.

Resources. The essential requirements are a tape recorder, stopwatch, blackboard, and duplicated problem sheets and response forms, samples of which are provided in the Student Manual. An overhead projector and video-recorder are optional.

Location. Any large classroom (preferably carpeted).

Prior knowledge assumed. Little prior knowledge of social psychology is required; some basic grounding in nonparametric statistics is helpful.

Special requirements. None.

Instructor's introduction

As a learning experience for students, this exercise is particularly useful in teaching the applications of a structured observational approach, and it raises many problems associated with classifying social acts or units of purposeful interactive behavior. In introducing the exercise to the students,

21

the instructor only needs to provide a little explanatory information. Although it is feasible to send discussants out of the room while observers are being initially instructed and trained (steps 1, 4–7 in the Student Manual), these students would be deprived of much of the educative function of the exercise. Our experience suggests that it does not matter much if the discussants know that their utterances and behavior are to be coded in certain ways, nor does it matter if they participate in the training exercise by coding their own interaction during the training problem. Expulsion from the classroom during these phases of the procedure carries its own problems in terms of creating disengagement from the exercise and a sense of feeling threatened and exposed when participating in the discussion tasks. Self-awareness is also likely to be heightened during the tasks, and this, to some extent, might detract from the involved and motivated discussions that are required for the test problems.

What matters more is that discussants should not at this stage have their attention specifically drawn to the nature and quality of their own contribution to the group, such as what types of reactions may be regarded as having positive emotional or negative emotional value, or how a group is typically supposed to proceed from the setting of its objectives to solution. Students do have ready access to this information from the introduction of the exercise in the Student Manual, so the discussants may not be naive about the functions that the categories are supposed to serve when they begin their discussion tasks. However, what knowledge they do have is unlikely to make them self-conscious about the nature of their social acts as long as the instructor does not draw attention to it.

From this it should be clear that the instructor's initial introduction must be kept short and very general, explaining in broad terms what the overall purpose of the exercise is as a training device and what kinds of general use such interactional analysis may have. When Bales' scale, or the modified version of it, is introduced in step 4 of the Student Manual, the instructor's explanations should be confined purely to definitions of particular categories and to problems of classifying behavioral acts, not to interpretations of the value of social acts.

Design and procedure

Duration

The exercise is very flexible and can largely be tailored to suit the time available. Typically it can last over two sessions of 3 hours each, or it can be compressed into one session. The essential difference between running it over one or two sessions lies in the inclusion of a training session, which can be omitted. The training procedure is somewhat time-consuming, but it serves to increase interobserver reliability considerably, as well as to familiarize observers with the categories they have to use, so its inclusion in the exercise is strongly recommended. For the purpose of providing full details, the exercise is treated in the Student Manual as consisting of two sessions.

If time demands that the exercise be compressed into one session, then the steps associated with the training problem (steps 3–7 inclusive, of Session 1) can be omitted. In this case the instructor should introduce the class to the coding categories and response forms after step 2, provide an explanation of their use, and then proceed with the practice problem (step 9). Although the observers are not in any sense trained, they will have some opportunity to express and share views about difficulties they experience in assigning codes.

Size of class and division of roles

Again, this is a very flexible exercise, and it is suitable for class sizes between 6 and 40. Since the class is divided up into a group (or groups) of "discussants" and "observers," the minimum number of discussants per group is 3, and the corresponding minimum number of observers is 3, one for each discussant. In practice it is desirable to have 4 or 5 class members in the discussion group(s) and then all the remaining members are observers, with up to 7 or 8 assigned to observe each discussant. The more observers there are recording the interactions of each discussant, the more unbiased their pooled data should be.

In the exercise outlined in the Student Manual, one group of 4 discussants is employed: The same discussants are used for the training problem, the practice problem, and the two test problems. There is no intrinsic objection to using different groups of discussants for each problem, but the advantage of keeping the same groups is that by the time they reach the test problems they are suitably warmed up to talking in front of the rest of the class, and comparisons of their profiles can be made between test problems 1 and 2. These problems were specifically designed as non-conflict and conflict situations, respectively.

If the class is really large, if the instructor has the assistance of graduate students, and if two rooms are available for use, the whole class can be divided in half, yielding two groups of discussants and observers to work through the problems in parallel. Comparisons between the styles of the two groups in tackling the same problems are then possible.

Some attention should be paid to the composition of the discussant group(s), and much depends upon the nature of the problem tasks selected: Test problem 2 (see appendix 4b in the Student Manual), which involves role-playing a family, requires father, mother, son, and daughter roles. There is therefore some advantage in deciding, before the exercise begins, whom to assign to be discussants, rather than just seeking for random volunteers: One criterion, at least, should be to select students who are talkative, well spoken, and self-confident; otherwise the discussion may bog down. It is advisable to have the names of one or two other suitable discussants in reserve in case of absence or genuine reluctance to participate.

Location

The exercise can be conducted in any reasonably large room or laboratory. In the interests of congeniality and the comfort of the discussants, it may be preferable to use a carpeted room rather than a bare laboratory. After initial briefing by the instructor, the seating has to be rearranged so that the discussants are seated around a table in the center of the room and encircled by the observers, who must occupy positions that give them a clear view of the discussants.

Resources and materials

Besides a stopwatch, tape recorder (or video-recorder), blackboard, and, optionally, an overhead projector, the only materials needed are duplicated problem sheets and response form matrices for collecting the group data, specifically described in the "Summary of Procedure" in the Student Manual. It should be emphasized that the problem sheets are just examples, and individual instructors may wish to modify the content of these or substitute their own problems entirely. The subjects used for the test problems and the training and practice problem are relatively immaterial; The guiding principles in relation to the selection of suitable test problems are (1) that solutions are possible, in the sense that a consensus can be achieved; (2) the problems are inherently debatable, requiring discussants to state their opinions and not requiring much factual information outside that provided by the instructions; (3) the problems are intrinsically interesting, to allow a sufficiently motivated discussion; (4) the instructions for one problem is divisive, in the sense that it sets the scene for a conflict of interests rather than a uniformity of interests. Hence test problem 2 was specifically designed to create conflict between the discussants, whereas test problem 1 was not.

The procedural steps outlined in the Student Manual are self-explanatory. In order to assess changes in the style of the discussion, it is suggested (in relation to the test problems – step 10 in the Student Manual) that the discussion periods for test problems 1 and 2 be divided into halves: Recordings of acts initiated during the second half cumulate in separate columns from those initiated during the first half. The time allotted for each discussion should be identical: between 12 and 20 minutes. This gives sufficient time for a reasonable amount of data to be collected without the discussants losing interest in the topic. It is important that they should be told in advance how long the discussion will last; it helps them pace their rate of progress. Observers can easily be informed unobtrusively when halftime has been reached.

It is also important that the two test problems should be given at the end of Session 1 and not held over to the start of Session 2. Much of the benefit of the warm-up for the discussants and training for the observers would be lost if the class came back cold to the test problems at the second session. Session 1 finishes after completion of the two test problems.

Follow-up discussion (Step 13)

On the assumption that the instructor has given very little information about the exercise at the start of Session 1, this is a suitable stage at which to tell the class in more detail about the Bales technique, the category system Bales uses, and the modified system employed in the present exercise. In the interests of simplification, the full 12-category system has been collapsed into 8 categories, which should give students a slightly easier task (see Table 4.1 of the Student Manual; an overhead slide of this might be useful).

The rationale for collapsing certain categories has been arrived at purely on the grounds of expediency, and this should be explained to the students. The categories "seems friendly" and "dramatizes" have been combined into "acts warmly," which is intended to encompass any act that serves to integrate or reward the group or bolster the status of others. Conversely, "shows tension" and "seems unfriendly" have been combined into "acts coldly" to convey the sense of antagonistic, critical acts likely to lead to increased tension within the group. In the task-related area, "gives/asks for opinion" and "gives/asks for orientation" have been combined into "gives/asks for direction." Although there is a distinction between opinion and orientation (information), the distinction is sometimes blurred in practice, and particularly in the role-play situations used in the problem tasks in this exercise, where group participants may have to invent some of the background details to the scenarios described. There is an inevitable loss to the analysis of the data resulting from this simplified category system, especially in terms of plotting changes in group process through time from problems of orientation to problems of evaluation and solution.

During the follow-up discussion, more can also be said about the general purpose of the exercise, in terms of the problems associated with classifying social acts, drawing from the introductory section to this exercise in the Student Manual.

5 Ethogenic methods: an empirical psychology of action

Rom Harré

Aim

The four exercises included all illustrate aspects of ethogenic methods. The first three are designed to introduce the student to the notion of systematically examining what people do and say for their social meanings and for the rules that govern them. These three exercises require the student to analyze ambiguous material for social meanings and encourage the student to learn to negotiate with others – including the original actors – to achieve a comprehensive interpretation. There are no right or wrong solutions in the interpretations. The purpose of the exercises is not to achieve consensus on what is portrayed in the material. The exercises give an opportunity to discuss how one might conduct nonmanipulative, collaborative research that is valid. The fourth exercise extends these three: The students generate their own accounts, over a lengthy period, of the development of a "friendship" and the stages and associated rituals that it passes through. This requires students to reflect upon their own experiences and the implicit rules that govern their own behavior.

Duration

Exercises 1 through 3 will take about 3 hours altogether, allowing time for discussion of interpretations and their relationship to any relevant social-psychological theories. Exercise 4 needs to be set up so that a "friendship diary" is written over a 2- to 3-month period, but the class session attached to it can be quite brief (2 hours), depending upon the level of detail in analysis.

Resources

No equipment is required, but each student will need a copy of the material for the exercises (see appendixes in Student Manual).

27

Analysis, and reporting conclusions

Students will require prompting to ask themselves the right sorts of questions when interpreting the material. Some are suggested in the Student's Manual. The problem for the teacher lies in collating these interpretations, since there are no easily quantifiable findings. To some extent this can be overcome by examining degree of preliminary consensus about rules and rituals involved, and answers to other questions, prior to any discussion. Individual independent analyses can then be compared with a final negotiated interpretation. The teacher can point out how idiosyncrasies of interpretation permeate or get lost in the final analysis. In the case of Exercise 3, the comparison of individual students' conclusions can be made with the model provided by Kreckel.

The students' reports of these exercises cannot be in the standard format because the methods are not those standardly used in social psychology. One solution is to write the report in the form of a comparison of the strengths and weaknesses of ethogenic methods with other methods, using the exercises as examples of the advantages and the problems.

Part II

Technique applications

6 Speech style and employment selection: the Matched Guise Technique

Peter Ball and Howard Giles

Aim

This exercise demonstrates a method used to study speech in interpersonal evaluation. Actual speech rate and pronunciation feature among the manipulations used, and perceived speech rate and pronunciation feature among the measures employed. Several points of methodology are introduced to students, besides research areas concerned with language, attitudes, and person perception. Potential applications in education and business are also discussed.

Method and analysis

In the first experiment, subjects hear someone talking about a job application and rate the candidate on four evaluative scales. Next they receive information about his or her success or failure when interviewed for the job and are required to estimate retrospectively several features of the person's speech. These data are analyzed for evidence of a retroactive halo effect on the perception of speech style.

This experiment provides practice for the main experiment, and facilitates establishing subject groups matched for evaluative response set. Subjects then play the role of employement agency personnel officers and listen to a job interview, different groups actually hearing the same speaker as candidate but in matched guises that differ in pronunciation and speech rate. Open-ended responses, in the form of written advice to the candidate and about him or her to another employment officer, are content-analyzed. These data, and ratings of the candidate's competence, pleasantness, and suitability for selected types of work are subjected to analysis of variance or to other suitable statistical treatments.

31

Prior knowledge assumed

No prior knowledge of social psychology or language/communication studies is assumed. In fact, naïveté can only increase the value of this exercise, which can be conducted in the traditional laboratory setting.

Resources

The only materials or resources necessary are a tape recorder (preferably of good quality), stimulus audiotapes, and questionnaires; the preparation time for the teacher is minimal. Before running the exercise for the very first time, two sets of short stimulus recordings need to be prepared carefully with the aid of three speakers, one of whom should be able to modify his or her accent realistically so as to make it more standard as well as more regional (or urban) than "normal." With the aid of the transcripts provided in the appendixes to Chapter 6 in the Student Manual, the recording session should take no longer than half an hour to an hour to produce satisfactory results and thereafter, of course, the tapes are available for all future occasions. Five pages of response sheets need to be duplicated for each subject, again according to the specifications laid out in the appendixes in the Student Manual, before the exercise is started on each time.

Duration

The entire exercise should be completed comfortably within a 3-hour session, but this could be reduced significantly if three assistants and three tape recorders, in three small rooms that are close together, also are available (at least for the first hour).

Subjects

The exercise requires 40 or more student subjects. Alternatively, one independent variable might be omitted from the experimental design. An absolute minimum of 10 subjects per cell of the main experiment, all unfamiliar with this research field, is recommended for a viable demonstration.

7 Recreational use of the street by boys and girls: an observational study

Antony J. Chapman and Frances M. Wade

Specification notes

Aim. This is an observational exercise in which information is collected as to how boys and girls of various ages use streets for recreational purposes. A simple category system is used for classifying activities. The underlying problem is an important and salient one associated with everyday activities: It is how to account for child pedestrian accidents and for the marked variation in accident rates associated with age and sex of children. Most child pedestrian accidents involve 5- to 9-year olds, especially boys. Specifically, the study examines whether trends in published statistics are a function of different amounts or types of street usage, with respect to (1) boys versus girls, and (2) 5- to 9-year-olds versus older and younger children.

Prior knowledge assumed. The exercise is suitable for students at the start of their course. It assumes little theoretical knowledge and only rudimentary expertise in descriptive and inferential statistics. From raw data, frequency counts are taken of the number of children of each age and sex category engaged in the following activities: running, walking, standing, sitting, talking, eating/drinking, active playing and passive playing, and location on the sidewalk or street. The ratio of observed boys to observed girls is compared to the resident population in order to assess the extent to which the sex difference in accident rates is reflected in the disproportionate use of the street by young boys. Percentage scores are used for examining age and sex differences in behaviors: Graphs are constructed, and inductive analysis is done by means of chi-square tests. Students can perform further analyses: for example, they can relate age and sex distributions of pedestrians to vehicle density for particular streets. It is valuable to have knowledge of reliability and validity concepts, and ethical issues

33

raised by the technique of observation can be discussed generally, as well as in relation to this particular study.

Duration. Two 3-hour sessions are required. The first session includes 60 to 90 minutes of fieldwork conducted outside of school (perhaps during school vacations). Between sessions students enter their data on collation sheets so as to facilitate the analysis and discussion of pooled data in the second session.

Location. The introductory session, and the data analysis and discussion, all take place in a laboratory or classroom. The collection of data is done in residential areas. Students are assigned predetermined routes to patrol, and the routes are within a locality in which the child population is known: Hence a locality may coincide with local public school (or school district) boundaries.

Procedure

The experiment is conducted in two consecutive sessions. In the first session, half the students begin by observing children (*Type A observers*), and half begin as observer-enumerators of traffic (*Type B observers*): The two types of observer are paired, and individuals switch roles halfway through their patrol. Each observer pair is assigned a small, unique sector of streets. Sectors should in combination comprise all streets in a geo-graphical area whose resident population can be determined fairly easily. For example, population information based on a census is available from the local school district. Schools are cooperative in research of this nature: They usually can supply details about district boundaries, and ages and sex distributions of children from their records. Local governments might be able to provide the same information.

The main resource for this exercise is a set of sections of a large-scale map divided into sectors, the number of sectors equaling the number of observer pairs. Prior to the first session the instructor annotates the sections with sector boundaries and route directions. A sector should comprise about 1 mile of streets, so that it requires approximately 30 minutes to patrol. When feasible, long shopping streets having many pedestrians are divided into two or more adjacent sectors, and in general the sectors should all include both quiet and busy streets. With a small number of students in the class, it may be possible to place all sectors on one large copy. However, there is much to be said for each observer pair receiving a unique map, with a single sector displayed and annotated; for example, observer pairs then have less excuse for encroaching upon another pair's sector, in part or in whole. But if this practice is followed, you may still want to produce a single map of the study area (by combining the various uniquely annotated maps): This would be useful for class discussion in the second session and hence would assist students in writing their reports. If some or all of the sectors are not within comfortable walking distance from the college, it may be necessary to underwrite student fares on public transportation or to obtain a van.

Before the first session the instructor prepares four sets of data sheets for distribution to students at the start of the exercise. These appear as appendixes 1 through 4 in the Student Manual and are referred to as the Pedestrian Data Sheet (10 per student), the Traffic Volume Sheet (5 per student), the Pedestrian Collation Sheet (3 per student), and the Traffic Density Collation Sheet (3 per student). Clipboards may be useful, but they do make the observers more conspicuous. A standard blackboard or overhead slide projector with transparencies and pens will be useful for the second session, which involves pooling observers' collated data.

Preparing students for the exercise

In order to minimize observer bias, *it is important that students remain blind to the precise hypotheses to be investigated.* Before they begin their observations, students need be told only that the project investigates children's recreational use of the street and that hypotheses relate to the "differential exposure to hazard" and "careless behavior" explanations of the age and sex patterns in pedestrian accident statistics. The specific predictions are as follows.

Prediction 1 is that boys' exposure to traffic hazard is greater than that of girls: Specifically, it is predicted that, excluding school journeys, the ratio of observed to resident children (the Observation Ratio, *OR*) is higher for boys than girls.

Prediction 2 is that boys engage in careless behaviors more than girls, namely, in running, active play, and activities in the street. Children in three age groups are observed (up to 4 years old; 5 to 9; and 10 to 14), and predictions are made (corresponding to predictions 1 and 2) consistent with rates for 5- to 9-year-olds being higher than for other children.

Hence, *Prediction 3* is that OR is higher for 5- to 9-year-olds than older children.

Prediction 4 is that careless behaviors are seen more commonly in 5- to 9-year-olds than older children. These two predictions are not extended to children under 4 because children in this age range are usually accompanied by adults.

The preobservation instructions given to the observers focus on the observational techniques, the category schemes, and the procedures to be followed. You will find it helpful to conduct a short pilot study yourself in one of the selected street sectors in order to gain familiarity with the scheme of behavioral categories detailed in the Student Manual. In this way you will be able to anticipate students' difficulties and worries.

Exercise objectives

As a training device this exercise serves to draw students' attention to several clusters of issues. It illustrates many of the problems routinely encountered in using virtually any system of categories for recording behavior. In this system, in combination with a number of mutually exclusive and specific categories (e.g., running and walking) are some less objective categories (such as active play or passive play). The two types of classification provide something of a contrast, and teachers may find that the latter are evaluated harshly or dismissively (e.g., on the specious grounds of being "unscientific"). These evaluations should be channeled into critical discussion; on the specific level, about tailoring the definitions to suit the research aims, and on the general level, about the nature of "science" and "scientific progress." The demand for unambiguous and discrete categories should be emphasized. The desirability of training observers should be raised too: For example, after a period of training at the task, we have found that observers claim that they are increasingly able to focus their attention and allow irrelevancies to stream past them. The exercise can be used to draw attention to problems of observer interference and bias. Even in the freedom afforded by a street, the observers may sometimes find that they have become entangled with their subjects. They may find that they have become an obstacle, perhaps causing pedestrians to step into the street. It is essential that observers not be biased in their choice of subjects. In particular, when there are many child pedestrians in sight, it is obviously vital to avoid any tendency to concentrate on those who are engaged in unusual or easily coded behavior: The simplest means of minimizing this form of potential bias is to observe the child, previously unrecorded, who is nearest.

At all stages of the project students handle data for themselves: They enter check marks on the data sheets, they convert those marks into numbers, they compile class data, and they perform statistical analyses (inferential and/or descriptive). This continuity aids the students' under-standing of how the data are transformed, and it helps them to extend the analysis for themselves. Two distinct types of data are yielded: nominal data (frequency scores) from the use of behavior categories, and ratio data from the head counts undertaken in calculating the sizes of the subsamples (for sexes and age groups). Of course, the nature of measurement changes as studies are "shaped" on the structuredness dimension, and by pointing to the ways in which increasing the structure of the categorization alters the type of data obtained, the exercise can be used to review the characteristics of nominal, ordinal, interval, and ratio scales of measurement. The use of simple binary-decision categories yield nominal data, as here, but if the design were to incorporate rating scales (e.g., of running speed) and duration measurements (e.g., of time spent running) the exercise would also yield ordinal and ratio data, respectively.

8   Social skills training

Paul Robinson and Peter Trower

Specification notes

Aim.   To demonstrate how relatively small changes in individuals' social behavior can dramatically affect their ability to have normal social interactions.

Prior knowledge assumed.   It is assumed that the students will have little or no knowledge of looking at elements of social behavior. A basic knowledge of experimental method and statistical analysis is assumed (including familiarity with the use of semantic differential scaling, although this can be omitted if it is new to the students).

Duration.   The exercise is expected to last approximately 3 hours, with a final discussion of results at a later date.

Location.   One large room or several smaller ones, depending on group size and equipment available.

Resources.   As many of the following as are available: stopwatches, event recorders, audio and video tape recorders. Variations are given for different equipment.

Special requirements.   None.

Running the exercise

The exercise involves two student actors enacting a series of four roughly scripted role-plays, while a group of other students record a number of observational measures. Besides checking out any equipment to be used, advance preparation involves selecting the actors, preparing scripts for them, and copying semantic differential forms. The exercise itself can then be run by the other students, following the manual with minimal supervision.

Organizing groups

The exercise requires a bare minimum of two actors and two observers. A reasonable working group would consist of two actors and four observers, plus someone to start and stop each role-play. It is best to split larger classes into groups of six to eight, so that data can be pooled for analysis. Otherwise, additional students can be assigned as extra observers.

Before the exercise, a pair of actors should be selected for each group. It is best if this is a mixed-sex pair, to avoid sex-role effects masking the behavior under consideration. The actors should also avoid reading through the exercise in the Student Manual, to minimize expectancy effects. After selection, actors are given scripts for their role-play and asked to familiarize themselves with the scripts, working individually – that is, each should read only his or her own script.

Materials

Role-play scripts

Actors will be asked to play a series of four role-plays, varying behaviors in a given social situation. To be effective, they should have guidelines describing the situation, indicating in general how individuals might react in such situations and noting the specific alteration of behavior required for each role-play.

The situation suggested here is that of sitting in a bar or coffee shop and being introduced to a stranger by a mutual acquaintance, then left to talk to him or her. Students probably are familiar with this kind of situation and with the normal pattern of interaction here. Variations can be selected from the list in Table A, but normal (nondeviant) behavior by both actors should always be included as one variation.

Thus for each group of students doing the exercise, intructors will need to prepare a set of eight scripts, four for each actor, each set incorporating variations of behavior. An example of a script is given in the appendix to this chapter of the Instructor's Manual. The set of scripts might cover variations such as the following:

A1   Actor 1: normal behavior
A2   Actor 2: normal behavior

B1   Actor 1: abnormal eye contact (0%)
B2   Actor 2: normal behavior

C1   Actor 1: normal behavior
C2   Actor 2: overlong pauses

D1   Actor 1: unclear hand over
D2   Actor 2: close body proximity

If a number of different groups is involved, the order of each group's variation should be staggered, to minimize order effects due to practice.

Other materials

Each working group will need eight copies of the scale given in appendix 1 of the Student Manual, which should be copied beforehand for use during the exercise.

Class follow-up

Besides the usual methodological issues raised by a research exercise, instructors might wish to develop class discussion afterward about the more specific problems involved in observing, analyzing, and recording social behaviors. Taking a more general approach, instructors could encourage discussion of the whole social skills approach to social behavior (e.g., Argyle & Trower, 1979) and of the practical implications it has in various problem areas (e.g., Bellack & Hersen, 1979).

Table A. *A Selection of possible variations in behavior*

1. Pausing too long before replying: For example, always count to eight before starting a speech.
2. Unclear hand over (finishing speaking to become listener): For example, always finish speech with an "um" or "er."
3. Abnormal eye gaze: For example, 0% or 100%.
4. Body proximity: moving closer to the other person than you feel is correct; continually moving your body toward them; touching them whenever there is a suitable opportunity (the sex of the individual carrying out this behavior will affect its outcome).
5. Using many questions that allow for only a short answer, such as "Where do you live?" "What do you do?" "What do your parents do?" "Do you have a car/motorcycle?" "Don't you think this place/party is awful?" If the person replying seems about to extend his or her answer, you should try to interrupt with another question.
6. Giving only brief answers to any questions asked, trying to be monosyllabic, and expressing few, if any, views on subjects.

References

Argyle, M., & Trower, P. (1979). *Person to Person: A Guide to Social Skills Training.* New York: Harper & Row.
Bellack A.S., & Herson, M. (eds.). (1979) *Research and Practice in Social Skills Training.* New York: Plenum Press.

Appendix. Role-play script

Setting. You are sitting in a bar and are introduced to a stranger by a mutual acquaintance who then leaves, and you try to carry on a conversation with the stranger.

Guidelines for your behavior. Ask a few questions to find out some background information on the other person, and then try to establish some common interest, or play it by ear in your usual way.

Behavior alteration required. While trying to act in the same way as you normally would, avoid *all* eye contact with the other person. It does not matter where you look, as long as you do not look at the person's face. The same thing applies to the other altered behavior: Act in your normal way, except for the specified behavior.

9   Person perception

Mark Cook

Specification notes

Aims.   To acquaint students with some of the methodological problems involved in measuring accuracy of person perception; to compare subjects' opinions about someone else's personality with an outside source; to test simple hypotheses about factors affecting accuracy of person perception.

Prior knowledge assumed.   Some knowledge of statistical analysis is desirable, although instructions and a formula for calculating rank order correlations are given. The instructor should be prepared to discuss with students the concepts of reliability, validity, and error of measurement in psychological tests.

Duration.   The exercise should take around 2 hours in all. This splits into an introduction and a period where students go out and collect data to analyze in class. The introductory session and analysis can be done in classes during two consecutive weeks, with the students collecting data in the intervening week. If students have groups of subjects arranged beforehand, then it is possible for the exercise to be run in one session.

Location.   Since the exercise is essentially a field study, all that is needed is a classroom for the introductory session and for analysis and discussion.

Resources.   Personality tests (e.g., Eysenck Personality Inventory); scoring keys; forms (supplied in the Student Manual); name tags; pens; calculators; statistical tables.

Special requirements.   None.

Running the exercise

Members of the class can run the exercise individually or in small groups, depending on class size and subjects available. Each experimenter group needs to arrange for a separate group of between 7 and 14 individuals to be available to them, and this should be checked in advance. The exercise itself involves students administering a personality questionnaire to subjects, then requesting subjects to engage in group discussion on a selected topic for a given time. At the end of discussion, subjects are asked to rank, on prepared forms, the other members of the group on given personality dimensions. Students then come back to the class to analyze the data.

Preparation

The instructor should ensure that all required materials are available ahead of the exercise. In particular, this means securing a sufficient number of copies of a suitable personality questionnaire, with a scoring key, and information about reliability and norms. It is suggested here that the Eysenck Personality Inventory (available from the Education and Industrial Testing Service, San Diego, CA, 92107) be used to give measures of extroversion and neuroticism. Instructors may wish to use other instruments, such as the California F Scale or the Rosenzweig Picture Frustration Study, if they prefer. In addition, the class will need copies of the Perceived Rank Order form and the Criterion Rank Order form (see appendixes 1 and 2 in the Student Manual). The other materials noted in the specification notes should also be ready for the class.

Students can prepare themselves fairly well by carefully reading the exercise in the Student Manual before carrying it out, but, if possible, it is useful for the instructor to explain the method and the hypotheses beforehand in some detail to the students before sending them out to collect the data.

Procedure

Preferably the instructor starts by giving preliminary instructions, as just described, and then supplies each experimenter or experimenter group with copies of the personality inventory and the Perceived Rank Order form. Class members then find their group, administer the inventory, set up a group discussion, and obtain ranking data from the subjects. Having obtained criterion data and perceived rank orders, students return to the class to score the inventories and construct the criterion rank orders, which are then correlated with perceived rank orders for each dimension under consideration, to give an index of accuracy. Further analyses are also carried out as indicated in the Student Manual. In this last stage, students may well need guidance from the instructor to help them understand their use of the materials, the meaning of the data obtained, and to assist with statistical analysis of the results.

Class follow-up

In class discussion, instructors can have students reflect on their experience of running the exercise and on the issues that it raises. Expanding on the exercise, instructors can bring the class to consider wider substantive and methodological issues involved in studying person perception and accuracy of judgments in this area (e.g., see Cook, 1982). If time permits, another useful topic to bring in here is that of personality tests, their validity, and their usefulness.

References

Cook, M. (1982). Perceiving others. In M. St. Davids and M. Davey (Eds.), *Judging People*. New York: McGraw-Hill.

10   Social dimensions of industrial bargaining

Geoffrey M. Stephenson and Maryon Tysoe

Specification notes

Aims.   The exercise is designed as a role-play experiment in intergroup processes in negotiation between union and management representatives. Negotiating instructions are varied to increase the salience of intergroup or interpersonal factors in negotiation.

Duration.   Two 3-hour sessions are required for the full version of the exercise to be implemented effectively.

Location.   A small room (or cubicle) is desirable for each pair, with a table and chairs; otherwise a large laboratory would be necessary.

Resources.   Cheap portable tape recorders, tapes, and microphones are required for each negotiating pair; stopwatches, writing paper, and pens should be available. Other negotiating information and scales in the appendixes must also be prepared and duplicated in advance.

Special requirements.   None.

The exercise

The exercise to be outlined in this chapter is based on the results of an experiment by Tysoe and Stephenson (unpublished) in which the orientation of the role-players was varied directly through the instructions concerning what attitude to adopt in the negotiation. The facts of the case, and the general instructions about what agreement should be secured, remain the same in both conditions. In the interpersonal condition, however, subjects are told additionally, before they start negotiating, that at the end of the negotiation they will be required to report on how their opponent

45

responded throughout the negotiation. In other words, they are instructed to be aware of the *other person's* thoughts and feelings. In the intergroup condition, on the other hand, subjects are instructed to be aware of how *their own constituency* would respond to what is being said. They are told that when the negotiations finish they will be required to write an account of how they think their fellow group members would evaluate what had happened in the negotiation. The former instructions emphasize the interpersonal dimension of the negotiation process, and the latter the intergroup dimension.

Using the material employed in this exercise, Tysoe and Stephenson found that the stronger case (in this instance, management's) prevailed more in the intergroup than in the interpersonal condition. They also discovered that women were more susceptible to the experimental manipulation than were men, a second aspect of the results that may be replicated in the current exercise, or at least controlled for in the composition of the groups.

How can you be sure that the intergroup and interpersonal instructions were effective? If subjects have followed their instructions, marked differences in the quality of interaction will occur, which will be reflected in analyses using modified versions of Bales' Interaction Process Analysis (IPA) (see Chapter 4 and Morley & Stephenson, 1977). In addition it will be found that negotiators are less identifiable as union or management representatives in the interpersonal than the intergroup condition. If time and experimental conditions permit, similar comparisons may be made between "all male" and "all female" negotiation pairs.

Schedule

Two sessions are required for the full version of the exercise to be implemented effectively. If only one is available, the analysis of the negotiation process may be excluded. However, role-playing may be completed, and an analysis of agreed settlements carried out and discussed satisfactorily, in one session. If 2 weeks are available, role-playing and transcription from the tape recordings would occupy the first session. The following week, outcomes, questionnaire results, and the "process" data would be analyzed and discussed.

Resources

It is desirable for each pair of negotiators to be able to record their discussion. (A cheap portable recorder is quite adequate for this purpose.

Cassette machines make transcribing easier). This is necessary if the process analysis is to be included in the exercise. If sufficient tape recorders are not available, then as many of the negotiations as possible should be recorded, distributed equally between experimental conditions. It is also advisable to have separate rooms (or cubicles) for each pair, but it may be possible to house a number of groups in a large laboratory, particularly if those groups are not to have their discussions recorded. In each negotiating room, in addition to the tape recorder, tape, and microphone, there should be a stopwatch placed on the negotiating table for timing the negotiation, spare writing paper and pens, and two chairs facing each other across the table. All participants should have previously been trained to use the tape recorder.

The items in appendixes 2 through 7 of the Student Manual should be reproduced as separate handouts in advance and, where different versions are required for different experimental conditions, these should be coded in some unobtrusive way.

To increase the realism of the exercise it is necessary to update the wage figures given in the background material. This can be done simply by adding a percentage roughly corresponding to the inflation rate. Since much of the detailed argument will center on equitable wage rates, it is not necessary to be pedantic about this, but it is important that the wage rates look reasonably realistic.

Aim of the exercise

The main manipulation in the exercise concerns intergroup versus interpersonal salience: The principal hypothesis is that the side with the stronger case – in this instance, management – will do better in the intergroup condition. The background material, or scenario, was written so as to favor the management side. In particular, the Townsford workers, being only in the middle range of skill, were relatively well paid and had generally been treated well by the company in the past, so that some sympathy for the company's present predicament would not have been unreasonable. Students should not have their attention drawn to this manipulation until after they have completed their negotiations and their questionnaires.

Procedure

Every member of the class can be expected to take part in this exercise as either a union or management representative. Allocation to union or management roles should be made according to performance on Stephenson's management–union questionnaire (see appendix 1 in the Student Manual), preferably administered and scored before the day of the exercise, to save time during it. Otherwise allocation can be random or based on personal preference. Random allocation at least disposes of one possible alternative explanation of differences that may be obtained between conditions: that is, an explanation in terms of personality differences. The disadvantage of this is the reduced face validity of the procedure.

A further random subdivision of subjects then needs to be made into "interpersonal" and "intergroup" conditions. So far as is possible, the ratio of men to women should be kept constant in all four groups (union interpersonal, union intergroup, management interpersonal, and management intergroup) that have been formed.

As indicated in the Student Manual, these four groups should, at the start of the exercise, meet separately to study their background material (appendixes 2, 3, and 4 in the Student Manual) and their negotiating instructions (see the appendix at the end of this chapter in the Instructor's Manual).

Twenty minutes is generally sufficient for this part of the exercise, including time for the instructor to answer questions about the material. Requests for further information about the company must, unfortunately, be politely refused, although technical terms and information must be explained if required. In order not to weaken the effects of the experimental manipulation (intergroup or interpersonal orientation), general discussion between participants should not be permitted during prenegotiation preparation.

Homogeneous (i.e., with the same negotiation instructions), same-sex (since previous studies have indicated differences in the orientation of men and women to this type of task) management/union pairs must then be formed. Each pair should be directed to their assigned position, where both members are given a copy of the negotiating rules (appendix 5), shown the required equipment (mentioned earlier), and seated opposite one another at the table. Each pair is given two final contract sheets (see appendix 6), one for issue 1 (pay increase) and another for issue 2 (paid vacation time). Once it is ascertained that the negotiating rules have been fully understood, the pairs can be left to themselves to negotiate a contract.

Additional advice on procedure

It is important that adequate time be allowed for mastery of the materials in groups, since some students will initially feel ill at ease with information of this kind. Students generally adopt a sensible and constructive approach and are usually very involved in the argument and debate. It is, of course, important for the instructor to be fully in command of the material and to be prepared to explain and defend the information provided. Some more knowledgeable students occasionally complain that insufficient background financial data are provided. This can be defended on the grounds that it is not feasible to provide more data in an exercise of this sort (and that in any case, factory-level negotiators in fact do quite frequently negotiate in comparative ignorance of the true state of their company's financial position). It can be also be emphasized that students are free to use their knowledge of the prevailing industrial relations climate in their negotiations.

It hardly needs to be said that the importance of the negotiation instructions (appendix in this manual) *must* be emphasized to the participants.

Procedures for 1-week and 2-week exercises

If only 1 week is available, then at this stage the class should be reconvened for a group analysis and discussion of the data already available; that is, the agreed outcomes and questionnaire results. When 2 weeks are available, the participants should at this stage obtain the necessary transcriptions, so that the *process* of negotiation can be analyzed (as well as the outcomes and questionnaire scores) the following week.

The interpersonal negotiations should differ in character from the intergroup negotiations. Ideally, a full transcript of each negotiation could form the basis of a comparison, using a suitable category system like Conference Process Analysis (CPA). In this exercise, just two hypotheses will be tested, using a simpler procedure:

- There will be more expressions of *agreement* in the interpersonal negotiations.
- The role (management or union) of negotiators will be more readily identifiable in intergroup than in interpersonal negotiations.

Data for the first hypothesis can be obtained by the pair replaying their negotiations and each member counting (by use of tally marks) the number of times he or she said something that justifies use of the CPA mode of *accept* (see appendix 8 in the Student Manual for definition and examples). The average acceptance rate per pair can then be determined by calculating the average number of accepts per minute of negotiations. This should be done during the first session.

Data for the second hypothesis comes from transcribed material. The pair should be asked to transcribe in detail 5 minutes' worth of negotiations, taken approximately from the middle of the negotiation. Copies of this should be given to the instructor for further preparation and use in class the following week.

During the interval between the two classes, the more enthusiastic participants should be asked to divide their transcripts into CPA acts and code them in terms of CPA categories. (For this purpose, students will need to refer to Chapter 10 of Morley & Stephenson, 1977).

Results

Analysis of outcomes

Does management do better in the intergroup than in the interpersonal condition, as has been predicted and previously demonstrated? That question can be answered by comparing the cost of the final settlement agreed by pairs in the two conditions. The cost should be lower in the intergroup condition. Each pair should calculate this by adding together the cost of the agreement on issues 1 and 2 to produce total cost scores. Conventional parametric statistical techniques may then be used to test the significance of differences between the conditions. For example, a t-test may be used to test the significance of the difference in total cost of the settlement in the interpersonal and intergroup conditions.

Besides examining the means, it will be fruitful to look for differences in the variability. An intergroup orientation is likely to constrain negotiators, so that a more limited range of outcomes is achieved than in the interpersonal condition, where negotiators may feel more at liberty to agree to what seems appropriate to them as individuals. This possibility should be examined. It should be noted that because the two issues are considered together as a package, it is not legitimate to treat each issue separately.

Deadlocks are more likely in the intergroup condition. The intergroup orientation is likely to lead to a greater intransigence on the part of the negotiators. The highly committed representatives may be moved to reiterate and emphasize their own position and opposition to alternatives, thus prolonging the negotiations in comparison to the interpersonal condition.

Analysis of postexperimental questionnaires (appendix 7)

As a check on the successfulness of the strength-of-case manipulation, the responses to question 7 may be examined. Of course, this check is not perfect, because it is likely that those who are seen to have "won" will be deemed to have had the stronger case. Nevertheless, there should be a general tendency for management to be seen as being in the strong position, and this is the view expressed by unbiased judges who do not know which role they will subsequently be asked to take.

Although there are unlikely to be differences between conditions in the responses to questions 1 and 2 (concerned with general satisfaction), if the experimental manipulation has been successful then there should be marked differences on questions 3 through 6. Negotiators in the intergroup condition should feel more "accountable" and "committed" and should have wanted to look "stronger." Analyses of scores (from 1 to 9) on each scale, using *t*-tests, should be carried out separately for those in management and union roles and for averaged scores from the pairs. This is because the general hypothesis (of greater commitment in the intergroup condition) is somewhat more likely to apply to those given the stronger (management) position.

Similar separate and combined analyses should be carried out for answers to question 6 on each of the scales contained there. There are likely to be overall differences between the interpersonal and intergroup conditions, with greater "tenacity," "unhelpfulness," and so on in the intergroup condition. However, this is most likely to occur for perceptions by union of management and for management's self-perceptions, given management's stronger case and greater likelihood of holding out for victory.

Analysis of negotiation process (Session 2)

The second session should begin with a consideration of *outcomes* before going on to analyze and discuss the results of the questionnaire. This will provide a good lead-in to a more detailed examination of the negotiation process. The questionnaire examines participants' perceptions of their behavior, whereas the process analysis aims to draw conclusions from more or less objective categorizations of that behavior.

While outlining the "additional procedure," earlier, we stated two hypotheses; that there will be more expressions of agreement in the interpersonal than in the intergroup condition, and that "role identifiability" will be greater in the intergroup than in the interpersonal condition. The first hypothesis may be tested simply using the CPA mode categorization *agree*, made by the participants themselves the week before. Methodologically this is not ideal, since the numerical judgments made by participants may be directly influenced by the experimental manipulation. In the context of a practical exercise, however, blind scoring is difficult to achieve. The agreement rate scores from the pairs in the intergroup and interpersonal conditions should be compared by using a *t*-test.

For the role identifiability hypothesis to be tested, it will be necessary for the instructor to have prepared material using the transcripts made by the participants the previous week. The four longest speeches by management (ignoring unsuccessful interruptions) and the four longest union speeches from each transcript should be typed up in random order, separately for each transcript. The experimental conditions and roles (management or union) should be coded, so as to be unidentifiable except to the instructor. In class, all the transcripts should be judged by each of the participants, every speech item being assigned either to the management or union role. The order in which transcripts are judged should be randomized, and the judges may be informed that the division of items between the roles is even. A score out of 8 (representing the number of speeches correctly identified) may then be obtained for each transcript as judged by each participant. An average score for each transcript can then be calculated and can be used to test for differences between intergroup and inter-personal conditions, using a *t*-test.

Other analyses may be carried out, if time permits. For example, there is the interesting question of sex differences in bargaining. There is evidence (Tysoe, 1979; Tysoe & Stephenson, unpublished) that women may negoti-ate differently, with respect both to what is said and what is decided. It may well be that women are more susceptible to the intergroup/interpersonal manipulation than are men, and this is a possibility that may be explored if there are sufficient data from the class, using all the indexes we have so far described.

Further analyses of the transcribed material can also be carried out by students separately and later brought together for subsequent group analysis and discussion. The intergroup condition is likely to yield a greater concern with what Bales termed task orientation of the "positive" kind and social-emotional behavior of a "negative" kind than in the interpersonal condition (which should foster more open-ended questioning and more positive social-emotional behavior).

Suggestions for use of Bales' IPA are given in chapter 4; Morley and Stephenson's CPA may also be employed. CPA was designed especially for use with negotiation groups, but it is more complex than IPA, making explicit some of the distinctions that are implicit and confused in Bales' system (for example, between "modes," the *manner* of exchange, and "resource," *what* is exchanged), and using special categories derived from analyses of interaction in bargaining. The system and its use are described fully in Morley and Stephenson (1977). It might also be useful to have the students code the protocols for the use of pressure (contentious) tactics. The work of Pruitt and Carnevale (1982) suggests that these are almost certain to be more pronounced in the intergroup than in the interpersonal condition. They measured the use of these tactics by first counting the number of statements involving threats, position commitments, put-downs, and efforts to persuade the other party to concede and then dividing by the total number of statements.

In relation to the use of bargaining teams, it is likely that, in contrast to individuals, they will most readily adopt an intergroup approach, which may decrease the likelihood that the intergroup/interpersonal manipulation will be effective.

Discussion

The findings should illustrate the importance of analyzing social behavior according to the interplay of its intergroup and interpersonal components. The experience of coping simultaneously with conflicting intergroup and interpersonal demands, even in role-playing, is one that is frequently found to be personally valuable, and it is worth finding time in general class discussion to allow students to comment on how well they felt they coped. It is also a central and neglected problem in social behavior generally, and some discussion of this should be initiated.

There are, of course, limits to the conclusions that can be drawn from such role-playing studies. For example, let us suppose that the results clearly demonstrate that the intergroup condition more frequently elicits victories for the party with the stronger case. Can this result be generalized? Unfortunately, this experimental design gives only management the stronger case. Maybe there is something about the managerial role or those people who are promanagement that contributes to this effect. Maybe in real life being truly responsible to a group either heightens the effects we have observed or conceivably diminishes them. Maybe the concept of "strength of case" does not apply straightforwardly in real life.

All these objections have some substance but should act only as a spur to further inquiry, both in the field and experimentally. The concept of role identifiability is itself based on analyses of real negotiations (Douglas, 1962; Morley & Stephenson, 1977; Stephenson, Kniveton, & Morley, 1977). Similarly, the decision to examine communications systems and "style" of bargaining was a result of observing remarkably consistent differences in the "quality" of negotiations in different factories (see Morley & Stephenson, 1977). This means that the theoretical issues examined in this exercise are directly relevant to industrial conclusions we might wish to tentatively infer. There is, however, a legitimate role for social psychology in the analysis of industrial relations problems that has been neglected in the past (see Stephenson & Brotherton, 1979). This exercise should illustrate both the potential usefulness of social psychology for industrial relations and, equally important, the contribution that analysis of such real-life contexts can make to theoretical issues in social psychology.

Conclusion

This exercise was designed to examine the effects of shifting negotiators' attention from the level of an interpersonal exchange to the role demands of negotiating an agreement on behalf of their parties. By doing so, it demonstrates (1) the potential *practical* value of research in social psychology for the understanding of industrial negotiations; (2) the *methodological* importance of using a paradigm that makes some attempt to capture the complexity of negotiations between groups in dispute and can, therefore, reveal the operation of such interpersonal and interparty orientations; and (3) the *theoretical* importance of distinguishing between the interpersonal and intergroup dimensions in interactions between members of different groups.

References

Douglas, A. (1962). *Industrial Peacemaking*. New York: Columbia University Press.
Morley, I. E., & Stephenson, G. M. (1977). *The Social Psychology of Bargaining*. London: Allen & Unwin.
Pruitt, D. G., & Carnevale, P. J. D. (1982). The development of integrative agreements. In V. J. Derlega & J. Grzelak (Eds.), *Living with Other People*. New York: Academic Press.
Stephenson, G. M., & Brotherton, C.. (1979). *Industrial Relations: A Social Psychological Approach*. New York: Wiley.
Stephenson, G. M., Kniveton, B. H., & Morley, I. E. (1977). Interaction analysis of an industrial wage negotiation. *Journal of Occupational Psychology*, 50, 231–41.
Tysoe, M. (1979). *An Experimental Investigation of the Efficacy of Some Procedural Role Requirements in Simulated Negotiations*. Unpublished Ph.D. dissertation, University of Nottingham.

Appendix. Negotiating instructions

There are four variations: two intergroup (management and union), and two interpersonal (management and union). They are as follows.

Intergroup management

PLEASE READ THESE NEGOTIATING INSTRUCTIONS CAREFULLY.

Attitudes toward your role. It is important for you to know what attitude to adopt toward your role. It is your task to come to an agreement with the union negotiator, an agreement that will be binding on both sides. In doing this I want you to be especially aware of the implications of what you are saying for your own party. At the end of the negotiation I shall ask you to say how you think your fellow managers will judge your performance as their representative. Remember that your opposite number is a union representative trying to get as much as he/she can for his/her own side. You must concentrate on the task you have been entrusted with; that is, to secure the agreement your side wants. Remember, you are accountable to your fellow managers.

Intergroup union

PLEASE READ THESE NEGOTIATING INSTRUCTIONS CAREFULLY.

Attitudes toward your role. It is important for you to know what attitude to adopt toward your role. It is your task to come to an agreement with the management negotiator, an agreement that will be binding on both sides. In doing this I want you to be especially aware of the implications of what you are saying for your own party. At the end of the negotiation I will ask you to say how you think your fellow union representatives will judge your performance as their representative. Remember that the other negotiator is a managerial representative aiming to get as much as he/she can for his/her own side. You must concentrate on the task you have been entrusted with; that is, to secure the agreement your side wants. Remember, you are accountable to your fellow union representatives.

Interpersonal management

PLEASE READ THESE NEGOTIATING INSTRUCTIONS CAREFULLY.

Attitudes toward your role. It is important for you to know what attitude to adopt toward your role. It is your task to come to an agreement with the union negotiator, an agreement that will be binding on both sides. In doing this I want you to be especially aware of the effect of what you are saying on the other person. At the end of the negotiation I will ask you to give an account of what happened from his or her personal point of view. Remember that the other negotiator is not just a union representative but an individual with a job to do. Try to understand how he/she might be feeling about things. Remember, you are both responsible people, and as such you are accountable to one another for the decision you reach together.

Interpersonal union

PLEASE READ THESE NEGOTIATING INSTRUCTIONS
CAREFULLY.

Attitudes toward your role.   It is important for you to know what attitude to adopt toward your role. It is your task to come to an agreement with the management negotiator, an agreement that will be binding on both sides. In doing this I want you to be especially aware of the effect of what you are saying on the other person. At the end of the negotiation I will ask you to give an account of what happened from his or her personal point of view. Remember that the other negotiator is not just a manager but an individual with a job to do. Try to understand how he/she might be feeling about things. Remember, you are both responsible people, and as such you are accountable to one another for the decision you reach together.

Part III

Problem investigations

11   Eyewitness accuracy

Ray Bull

Specification notes

Aim.   To determine whether males or females are the more accurate eyewitnesses. Further optional hypotheses concern the effect of sex of target and the duration of interaction on eyewitness recall.

Prior knowledge assumed.   Little or no prior theoretical knowledge is required, but a basic grounding in simple statistics may be necessary.

Duration.   This exercise can be conducted within 3 hours, or it can be made more complex and thus require two 3-hour sessions.

Location.   The data gathering is not complicated, and it is conducted in any public place where there is considerable pedestrian traffic.

Resources.   No special equipment or resources except a set of *t*-test tables are required.

Running the exercise

This exercise can be carried out by the students, working by themselves from the Student Manual. No advance preparation by the instructor is necessary.

Points for class discussion

The main issues relating to the exercise are noted in the Student Manual. Besides expanding on the points raised there, you might want to develop a class discussion about the practical and theoretical problems involved in carrying out field research, as compared with laboratory research, and relate these in turn to the question of researching into real social problems.

59

12   Attribution processes

Mansur Lalljee

Specification notes

The exercise described in this chapter is designed to test Kelley's hypotheses concerning the influence of consensus, consistency, and distinctiveness information in making causal attributions, within the context of attributions for success and failure. In keeping with much of the research on attribution processes, a questionnaire consisting of brief descriptions of hypothetical events is proposed as a way of pursuing the problem. Two different dependent variables are suggested: rating scales of attribution to personal and situational causes, and the respondents' open-ended explanations about why the event occurred. The chief value of the exercise is that students are introduced to the methodological problems involved in drawing up a questionnaire and that they gain some experience of content analysis and in conducting a factorial, repeated-measures analysis of variance.

Aims.   (1) To teach students how to structure stimulus material and design questionnaires to test hypotheses; (2) to permit teaching and practice of analysis of variance; (3) to introduce students to content analysis.

Prior knowledge assumed.   None.

Duration.   Between $2\frac{1}{2}$ and 3 hours.

Location.   Only one room is necessary, provided that students are able to confer in groups of about four.

Resources.   Each student will need a copy of the questionnaire included in appendix 1 and of the coding categories for the content analysis included in appendix 2.

60

Special requirements. none.

General requirements

The exercise can be completed in $2\frac{1}{2}$ to 3 hours, including the calculation of means and standard deviations with an appropriate calculator. Unless a calculator programmed to perform the relevant analysis of variance is available, the complete statistical analysis will have to be done outside class time. The students themselves will serve as subjects for the exercise. Each student will need one copy of the questionnaire in appendix 1 and one copy of the content analysis coding sheet in appendix 2. The exercise can be conducted in one room, and for most of the time students can sit at tables, filling in the questionnaire, reporting data, and commenting on aspects of the exercise. For part of the time students will be asked to confer in groups of about 4 to discuss aspects of the content analysis. It is assumed that there will be about 30 students in the class. Smaller numbers will make data collection easier and the exercise shorter. An alternative format is suggested to deal with larger numbers.

Questionnaire

The questionnaire consists of 24 items. Six items refer to intellectual events, and six to interpersonal events. The intellectual items are instances of a history examination, a geography paper, a biology lab test, a cross-word puzzle, an anagram test, and a radio quiz. The interpersonal items are instances of attempts to impress, encourage, gain respect, reassure, interest, and dominate.

Within each type of item, half were randomly assigned to successful outcomes and half to unsuccessful outcomes. All the 12 items appear twice, once with high-consensus, high-distinctiveness, or high-consistency information, and once with low-consensus, low-distinctiveness, or low-consistency information. The final order of the items in the questionnaire was randomly determined, with the constraint that the two instances of the same event do not occur in succession.

Thus there are three independent variables: type of information, success/failure outcome, and event type. The design is a 2 × 2 × 2 factorial, with repeated measures across all factors. For each item, subjects are asked to provide (1) open-ended explanations and (2) ratings of attributions to personal and situational causes.

The general structure of the session will be as follows:

1. Administration of questionnaire. This will be done in two parts: First the subjects are asked for open-ended explanations; when this is completed they make attributions of causality on a 7-point rating scale, attributing causality to personal or situational causes (approximately 30 minutes).
2. Brief exposition of the ideas and background to the study, followed by discussion of the design of the study and the items on the questionnaire (approximately 30 minutes).
3. Analysis of ratings of the consensus information (approximately 30 minutes).
4. Introduction to the content analysis, and carrying out content analysis in groups of four (approximately 30 minutes).
5. Statistical analysis of the results of the distinctiveness items (approximately 30 minutes).

Seating arrangements should be such that students can fill in a questionnaire but will also be able to divide into groups of four for the content analysis. The instructions to the class and the suggested questionnaire are in appendix 1. It should be made clear to the students that they should finish part 1 of the questionnaire (the open-ended explanations) and then pause. They should not look at the second part until the entire class has completed the first part, since knowing that they will be asked to make ratings of attributions of causality to personal situational causes may influence their own explanations.

The administration of the questionnaire should take about 30 minutes. This should be followed by a brief exposition of the theory and a detailed discussion of the design of the questionnaire.

Data collection, analysis, and results

The class will have two sorts of data: ratings of attributions of causality, and open-ended explanations about why the event occurred. Analysis of each type of data should be performed separately.

Data from the rating scales can be used to test the hypothesis concerning consensus information, and data from the open-ended explanations can be used to test the hypothesis concerning distinctiveness information. The effects of outcome and of event type can be analyzed in both cases. These analyses can be demonstrated in class, and the data from the consistency information can be used for the students to analyze independently, if this is thought advisable.

After discussion of the theory and of the design of the questionnaire, the instructor should tabulate the data for the consensus-information items on the board. A data sheet is presented in Table 12.1.

If the class consists of about 30 students or fewer, it is relatively easy to have each student read out his or her results and for the instructor to put them on the board. Students can copy the results into their own notebooks as they are being tabulated, and they will therefore have the data to perform their own analysis independently. If there are more than 30 students in the class, tabulation of the data from all the students may not be possible. The class can then be split into two groups, and the instructor may want to treat the type of event as a between-groups factor. In that case, the data from some students can be used for the intellectual items, and the data from other students for the interpersonal items. Thus, some data from all members of the class can be used.

The data can be collected and tabulated in about 30 minutes, and some of the students can be asked to calculate the means and standard deviations for each of the main effects and the interactions. If the main hypothesis is confirmed, the average of the scores for high-consensus items should be higher than the average for low-consensus items. The interaction between outcome and event type can also be readily examined. The average of the scores for intellectual/failure items should be the highest, that for the intellectual/success items the lowest, and those for the two set of interpersonal items should be in between.

After completing analysis of the rating scales, students should turn to the content analysis of the open-ended explanations. They should be divided into groups of four for the coding of their responses. They should first familiarize themselves with the coding scheme in appendix 2 and then proceed to code their own responses. They should code their responses *not* on the questionnaire but on a separate sheet, since each questionnaire will be coded by several students. When a student has completed the analysis of his or her own data, that student should *exchange* the questionnaire with one of the other members of the four-person group and independently code the responses of that other student. Next the two students should discuss the coding of their two questionnaires, checking their level of agreement and resolving disagreements. This will enable them to have some preliminary practice before they code data that will be statistically analyzed. When the pair of students has completed discussion of their own two questionnaires, they should then exchange questionnaires with the other two members of their group. They should independently code the responses of the two questionnaires, and, when this is completed, work out the percentage of items on which they agreed. They should then arrive at agreement for the remaining items. These data will be analyzed statistically.

The instructor should first ask how many pairs achieved agreement on at least 90% of the data, and then how many achieved agreement on at least 80%. The causes of the difficulty and limitations of the coding scheme can be considered. This can be done through asking what responses were particularly difficult to code, and why. A tabulation should be kept of the number of disagreements per item; items that accumulate large numbers of disagreements require modification in wording or clarification of their code.

The data should be examined for the effects of distinctiveness information. One simple way of analyzing the results is by dichotomizing the data in terms of whether or not a person explanation is provided and then performing a $2 \times 2 \times 2$ analysis of variance. The relevant data sheet is presented in Table 12.2. If the main hypothesis concerning the effects of distinctiveness information is confirmed, scores for high distinctiveness should be higher than scores for low distinctiveness. The interaction between outcome and type of event is similar to that expected in the case of consensus information.

If desired, the effects of consistency information can be tabulated as shown in Table 12.3.

13   An aspect of prejudice

Glynis M. Breakwell

Aim

The aim of this exercise is to introduce students to the experimental investigation of intergroup dynamics – particularly that aspect of prejudice that is associated with devalutation of an out-group's products – and to the way in which this is affected by the manipulation of group memberships.

Prior knowledge assumed

No prior knowledge of this area of the literature is assumed. The exercise is an ideal vehicle for introducing students to analysis of variance techniques in experimental design, but students with lower levels of statistical expertise will be able to treat the data generated more simply.

Duration

The exercise can be divided into three parts: collection of data (1 hour); collation of results and directions for analysis (1 hour); and discussion of method and results (1 hour). If preferred, the last part can be done in a separate session after students have had time to complete the analysis individually.

Materials

No special resources or facilities are required. Before the experiment is done, two sets of rating scales need to be produced, one for the cover story, one for the judgments subjects make about group products. The cover story suggested assumes that the experimenters will pretend to monitor communication patterns in the groups during the time the task is completed; they will do this using the cover story rating scale. The format for the rating scale to be used by subjects is given in the appendix to this exercise in the Student Manual. There must be as many copies of this rating scale as there are subjects. Collation tables for entering the results (Table 13.1 in the Student Manual) should also be prepared before the experiment is done, so that each student can have a copy of the raw data for analysis.

Subjects

In this exercise, it is preferable not to have class members act as subjects, since the effectiveness of the manipulation depends upon the subjects' belief in the cover story. Using class members only as experimenters also has the advantage that they can be involved in the choice and production of the cover story, rating scales, and materials.

Additional Literature

The chapter in the Student Manual reviews much of the recent literature in the area, with a sharp eye to methodological and interpretative problems. See especially S. Hinkle and J. Schopler (1985), "Bias in the evaluation of ingroup and outgroup performances," in S. Worchel and W. Austin (eds.), *The Social Psychology of Intergroup Relations*, revised ed. (Chicago: Nelson Hall).

14 Crowd panic: competing and cooperating in groups

Robin Gilmour

Specification notes

Aim. To examine some of the determinants of crowd panic behavior; to see how far it is possible to set up in the laboratory a meaningful experimental analogue of a large-scale social phenomenon.

Prior knowledge assumed. Little prior knowledge on the part of students is assumed. Some basic appreciation of the experimental approach in social psychology would be helpful; the exercise can be used to develop this.

Duration. The exercise can be conducted within a single 3-hour period.

Location. One large room or two smaller rooms would normally be required. The exercise can be carried out using one fairly small room, if space is limited.

Resources. Watches, notebooks, and a reward system. For the last it would be useful if a reasonable sum of money were available for this purpose, though the exercise can still be run effectively with small amounts of money or an inexpensive substitute such as candy (see the "Resources" section of the Student Manual for discussion of the issues here).

Special requirements. Narrow-necked chemistry jars. A number of cones will have to be made for the exercise (see main "Resources" section of the method in the Student Manual for details).

Running the exercise

This is pretty straightforward. Advance preparation is mainly concerned with making sure the materials required are available. The only equipment that needs special attention is the jars and cones that will have to be acquired in advance or made up ready for the exercise: Details of these are given in the "Method" section of the Student Manual.

The other advance preparation relates to subjects. The exercise requires at least two groups of five or six subjects, plus two or three experimenters, per group. If subjects from outside the class are easily available, it is best to use these and have the class members running the exercise as experimenters. Otherwise, some of the class can be designated to act as subjects, and if this is to be done the class should be allocated to their roles as experimenters or subjects in advance, and those acting as subjects should be asked *not* to read through the exercise beforehand, so that they can maintain the part of "naive" subjects. Sessions with the subjects should be scheduled so that the experimenters will have time to set up equipment first and familiarize themselves fully with the procedure, which can be done in about 1 hour.

In addition, the student experimenters need to know which condition they will be running. They can decide this by agreement among themselves or can simply be assigned to conditions. Once materials, room, and experimental conditions have been assigned, students can be left to carry out the exercise with minimal supervision from the instructor.

Class follow-up

The exercise can be run as a self-contained experiment, with students following the Student Manual. However, there are a number of issues involved that can be brought out in class discussion and followed up if desired.

1. At the specific level, it is useful for the class to discuss their experience of carrying out the exercise and to pick up on points of practice that raise questions concerning experimental design. The existing design can be critically evaluated and improvements suggested: The Student Manual points out some of the problems here, and this can be used as a basis for discussion.

2. The data produced by the exercise are particularly interesting in that they are crude, but typically show large differences that seem "obviously" significant yet are difficult to subject to statistical proof. This allows the instructor to raise issues about measurement in social psychology and about the use and problems of statistical tests.

3. On a broader methodological level, the exercise here and the Mintz experiment on which it is based can be used to introduce issues about experimental approaches in social psychology. The instructor can open up

the whole debate about the value of the traditional experimental approach (e.g., see Harré, 1980) or can focus more directly on questions such as the validity of trying to bring complex social behaviors into the laboratory by modeling certain features. Criticisms of artificiality in research can also be addressed, since the actual exercise of pulling cones out of jars seems about as far removed from crowds in panic as it is possible to get, yet experience of doing the exercise suggests that it has more experimental realism than at first appears, so perhaps we can get students to think more carefully about the question of artificiality and its importance.

4. Substantively the exercise can introduce considerations about "rational" and reward-based analyses of social behavior, and this can be used to lead into the whole area of social exchange theory and its applications in social psychology (cf. Baron & Byrne, 1987, Chapter 10).

References

Baron, R.A., & Byrne, D. (1987) *Social Psychology*, 5th ed. Boston: Allyn & Bacon.
Harré, R. (1980) Causes for persuasion. In R. Gilmour and S.W. Duck (Eds.), *The Development of Social Psychology*. New York: Academic Press.

15   Norms and roles in the small group

Specification notes

Aim.   The purpose of this exercise is to teach students to interrelate what
they have read about small group behavior in texts with the behavior of
a particular small group to which they belong; to demonstrate the inter-
connections between social norms and social roles; and to illustrate how
data collection can be used not only to study behavior but also to create
opportunities for changing it.

Prior knowledge assumed.   Some prior instruction on research methods
is assumed. Familiarity with Asch-type conformity studies and the use of
rank correlation coefficients is an advantage.

Duration.   The exercise requires 2 to 3 hours to complete.

Location.   Any room large enough to seat the members of the class will
suffice.

Resources.   A blackboard is needed. Copies of one handout and one
questionnaire must be prepared in advance.

Special requirements.   It is best to conduct the exercise as late as possible
in the semester or year within which the class occurs.

Materials

The materials required are presented as appendixes 1 and 2 in the Student
Manual. The number of questionnaires prepared in advance should be
twice the number of students in the class. This enables class members to
submit their responses in a manner that preserves their anonymity, while at

70

the same time leaving them with a record of their own responses, which they will need at a later stage in the processing of the data. Only one copy of the handout is required for each student.

Other issues

Deciding whether to use this exercise.   As in the case of all action research projects, it makes sense to initiate this type of data collection only if you, the professor, are open to the possibility of making changes in the manner in which the class is conducted. There is no way of knowing in advance exactly what issues or discontents will be brought to the surface by this exercise, but the fact that they are publicly shared creates an impetus for possible change. There is no reason why this should prove unmanageable, and actually it may well turn out to be helpful to you in conducting the class, but it is wise to think out in advance what issues are likely to come up and how you would respond to them. It is important to leave enough class discussion time for these issues to be resolved. Some care is also required in conducting this exercise in a manner that is not personally intrusive to class members, particularly to minorities.

Timing within the course.   Since this project is concerned with investigating the emergent structures of groups, as much time as possible should be allowed to permit those structures to emerge. This means that the project should be scheduled as late as possible within the term. If there is some continuity of class membership from term to term, then a later term would be preferable. It would not, however, be impossible to do the exercise in a relatively early term. Doing it early rather than late would probably result in finding lesser degree of normative consensus and the norms that did apply would probably be less distinctive and more characteristic of those found in student groups in general.

Procedure.   When the handout has been distributed to the class, and the class is discussing which items to include on the list as possible norms, do not permit any taking of votes or straw polls at this stage, since they might very well bias each individual's later responses to the questionnaire.

When the list of potential norms has been decided, the group is next required to select an appropriate demographic variable whose relation to the norm structure can be studied. In some cases it may be appropriate for you to decide in advance what this dimension will be. You should do this if your knowledge of the group's earlier history makes you think either that they will have difficulty deciding or that some earlier conflict between different subgroups might be reopened in a manner that would leave a minority group exposed or vulnerable. What you need is a dimension that divides the class fairly evenly.

This exercise provides a range of choices as to whether the data will be analyzed in a predominantly qualitative or a quantitative way. It also raises the possibility that the exercise will uncover issues concerning the group's shared history or aspects of how the course is conducted that will require discussion time to resolve. Since there are various possible choices, it is not possible to specify an overall schedule, but it would be valuable for you to set some targets for your particular class and to help them stick to them.

Further reading

Paulus, P.B., ed. *Psychology of Group Influence*. Hillsdale, N.J.: Erlbaum, 1980.

Index

accident rates, children's, 33
action, empirical psychology of, *see*
   ethogenic methods exercises
attitude measurement exercise: calculating
   reliability and, 19; class discussion and, 20;
   individual differences in working speed,
   18; introductory lecture, 17–18; ogive
   graph and, 19; phases of, 16–17;
   preparation for, 17; procedure for, 17–20;
   resources, equipment, and supplies
   needed, 16; scoring procedure and, 19;
   Thurstone procedure and, 18, 19; time
   required, 16; validation problems and, 19
attribution processes exercise: data
   collection, analysis, and results, 62–64;
   general structure of session for, 61–62;
   Kelley's hypothesis and, 60; questionnaire
   for, 61–62; resources needed, 60;
   statistical analysis and, 61; time required,
   60

Bales' Interaction Process Analysis, 21, 46,
   52; introducing students to, 22
bargaining, *see* social dimensions of
   industrial bargaining exercise
behavior: problems in recording, 36–37;
   social, 69; variations in, 40, 41

child pedestrian accidents, *see* recreational
   use of streets exercise
competing and cooperating in groups, 67–69
conflicting intergroup and interpersonal
   demands, 53
courtroom witnesses, *see* eyewitness
   testimony exercise
crowd panic, 67–69

employment interviewing, *see* employment
   selection and speech style exercise;
   personnel interviewing exercise

employment selection and speech style
   exercise, 31–32
ethogenic methods exercises, 27–28
eye contact, 41
eyewitness testimony exercise, 59

friendship, development of, 27

groups: competing and cooperating in,
   67–69; norms and roles in small, 70–72

industrial bargaining, *see* social dimensions
   of industrial bargaining exercise
industrial relations, social psychology and,
   54
intergroup dynamics, 65–66
interpersonal evaluation, 31–32; *see also*
   personnel interviewing
interviews for jobs, 11, 12–15, 31–32

job interviewing, *see* personnel interviewing
   exercise; speech style and employment
   selection

management-union questionnaire, 48
matched guise technique, 31–32
memory, *see* eyewitness testimony exercise

negotiation, 51–53; *see also* social
   dimensions of industrial bargaining
   exercise
norms and roles in small groups exercise,
   70–72

ogive graph, 19

personnel interviewing exercise: closed-
   circuit television for, 13–14; equipment
   and supplies required, 11, 12, 13–14;
   person evaluation models and, 15;